Little Q™

Getting Ready For Reading

A Little Q™ Electronic Workbook

Illustrated by Terry Anderson

PRICE STERN SLOAN
Los Angeles

The Fun Way to Start Learning

This book is specially designed for use with the **Little Q Electronic Answer Wand.** When the Little Q answer wand is moved over the pages of a **Little Q Electronic Workbook** it detects correct and incorrect answers and responds with "right" or "wrong" sounds and lights.

The Little Q Electronic Learning System has been created to equip the 3 to 6-year-old with the all-important basic skills, and is simple enough for children to use all by themselves. The bright, easy-to-handle Little Q wand plus the colorful, interactive **Little Q Electronic Library** of books provide a structured learning environment for children as they begin to understand reading and mathematics.

Little Q has reinvented the 3 Rs to help children learn in the most efficient way.

Recognition Children recognize concepts by associating pictures, words and numbers.

Repetition Activities are designed to be done again and again, reinforcing ideas and helping children remember what they learn.

Reward The "beeping" and "buzzing" sounds and flashing lights make little children feel terrific.

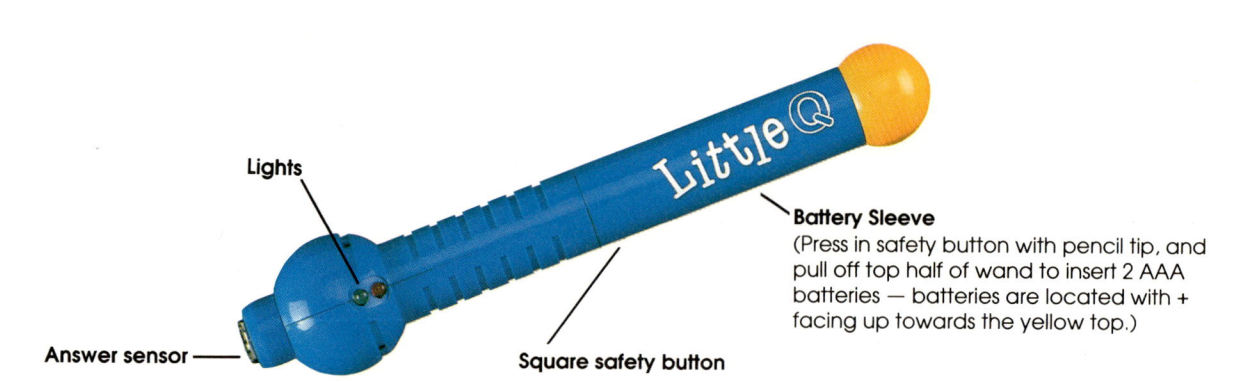

Lights

Battery Sleeve
(Press in safety button with pencil tip, and pull off top half of wand to insert 2 AAA batteries — batteries are located with + facing up towards the yellow top.)

Answer sensor

Square safety button

Concept Roger Burrows *M. Ed.,* **Educational Consultants** Deborah Christine *M. Ed.* & Stevie Mack *M. Ed.*
Book Development, Design and Production Morgan-Slade & Associates, Menlo Park, CA

Copyright © 1988 by Price Stern Sloan, Inc. All rights reserved under International and Pan American Copyright Conventions. No part of this publication may be reproduced, stored in a retrieval system, or transmitted in any form, or by any means, electronic, mechanical, photocopying, recording or otherwise, without the prior written permission of the publisher.   ISBN: 0-8431-3135-7
Published by Price Stern Sloan, Inc. 360 North La Cienega Boulevard, Los Angeles, California 90048.   1 2 3 4 5 6 7 8 9 0
Questron® and Little Q™ are a trademarks of Price Stern Sloan, Inc. USA. U.S. Patent 4,604,065; U.S. Patent 4,627,819; U.S. Patent Pending.
Printed in the United States of America.

Try Little Q here

You can **press** or **track** answers with Little Q!

PRESS
Press Little Q firmly on the rectangle and triangle below

CORRECT

INCORRECT

Green light and "beep"

Red light and "buzz"

TRACK
Keep Little Q pressed on the page as you track through the answers

Start Tracking →

b

Stop tracking ★

Little Q's batteries need replacing when it reads all answers as correct

find the letters

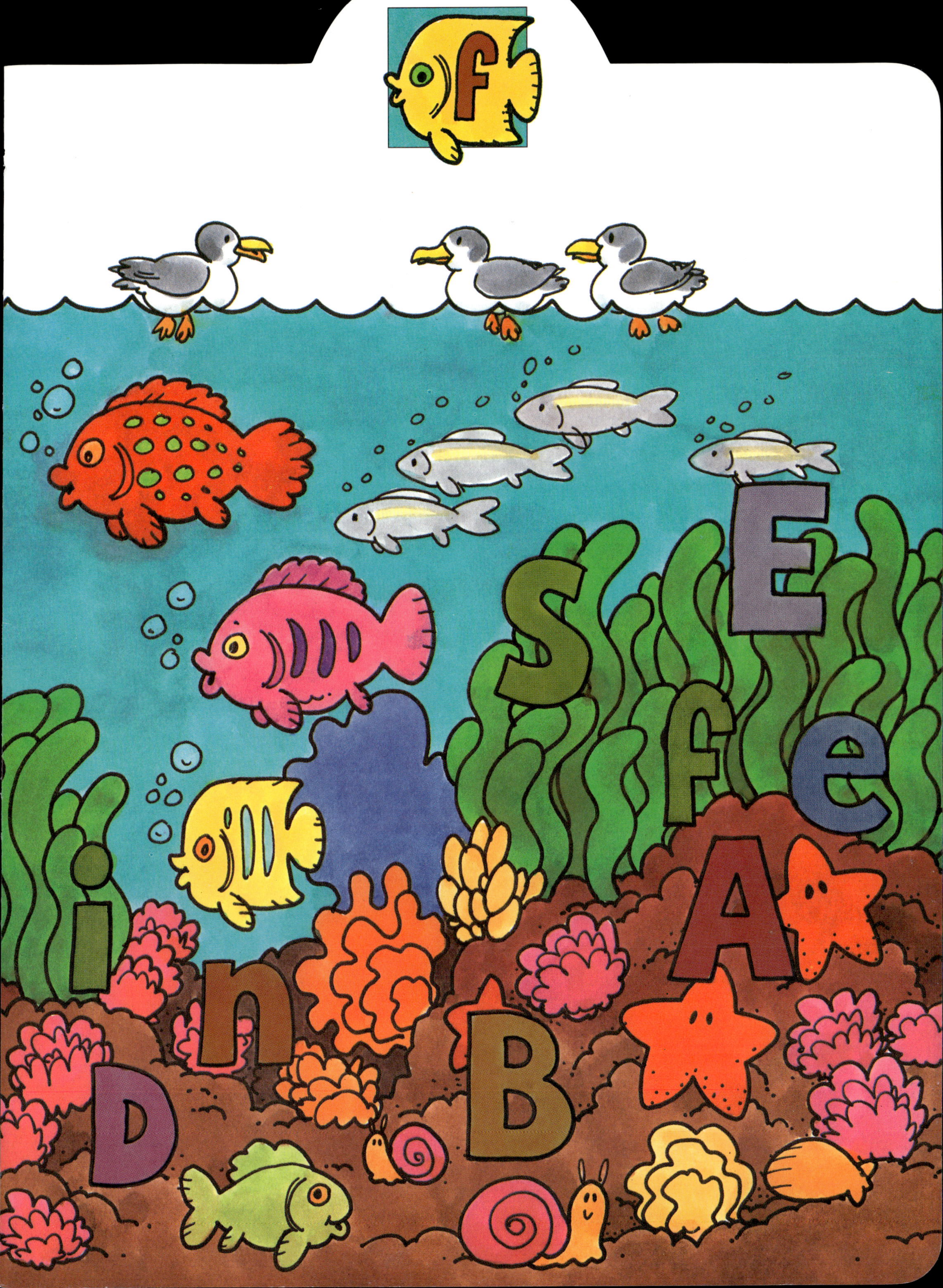
f
E
S
f
e
A
i
n
D
B

match

match

animals that fly

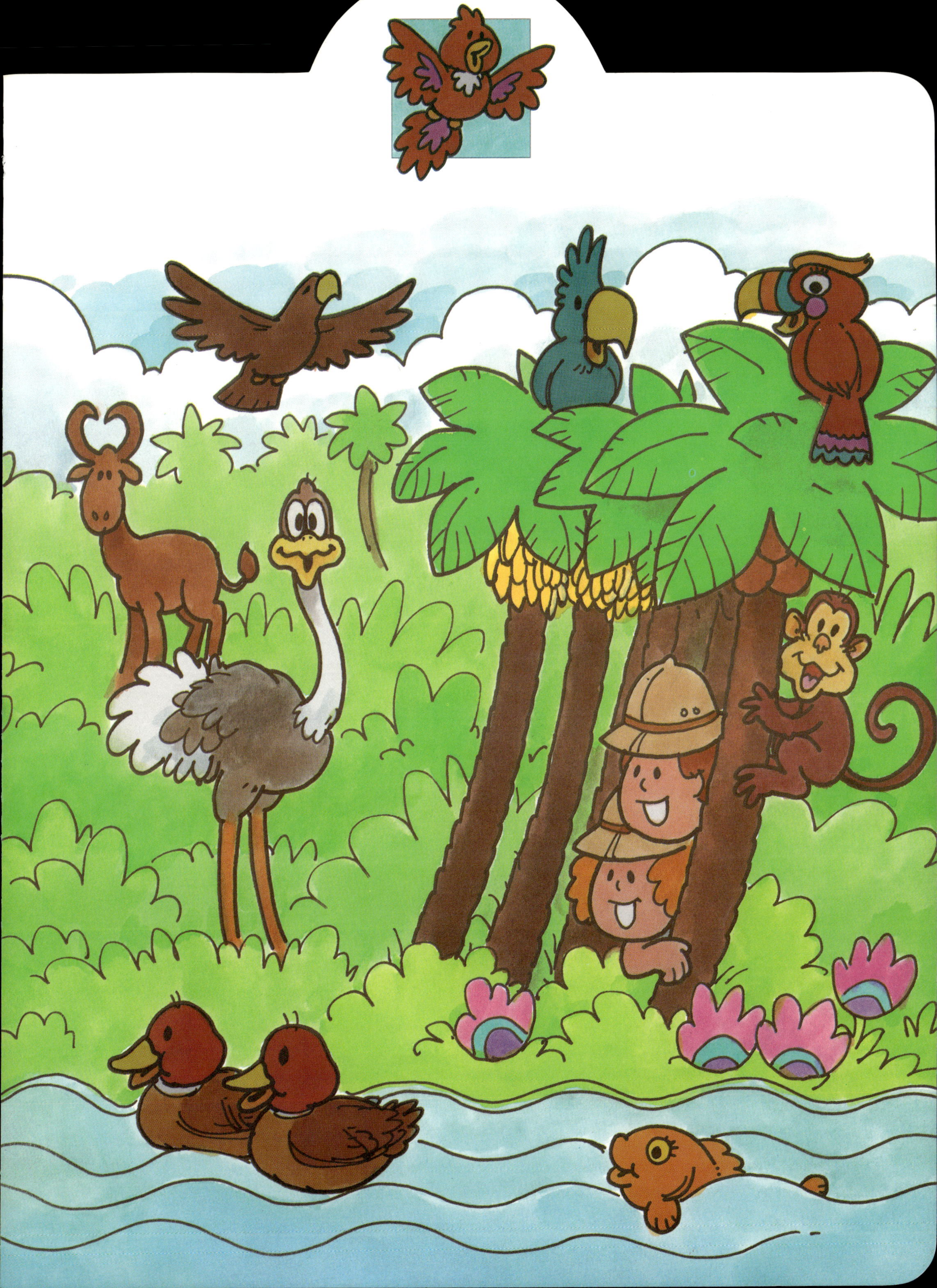

what's wrong?

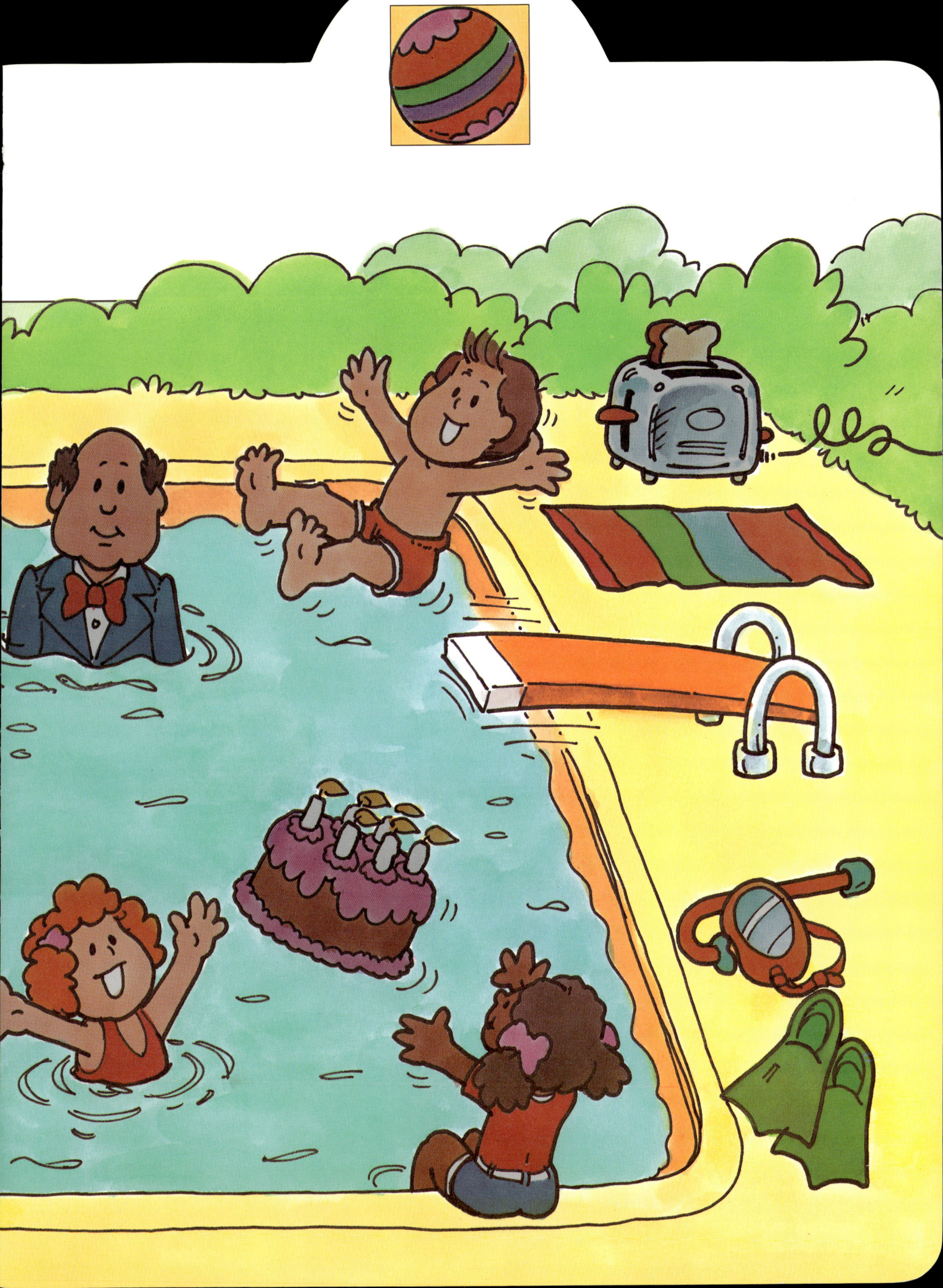

complete

complete

rhyme

lamp
cat
chair
door
hat
dog
cup
mat
ball
bat

cap
hat
clock
cane
bat
rat
cat
rug

things with wheels

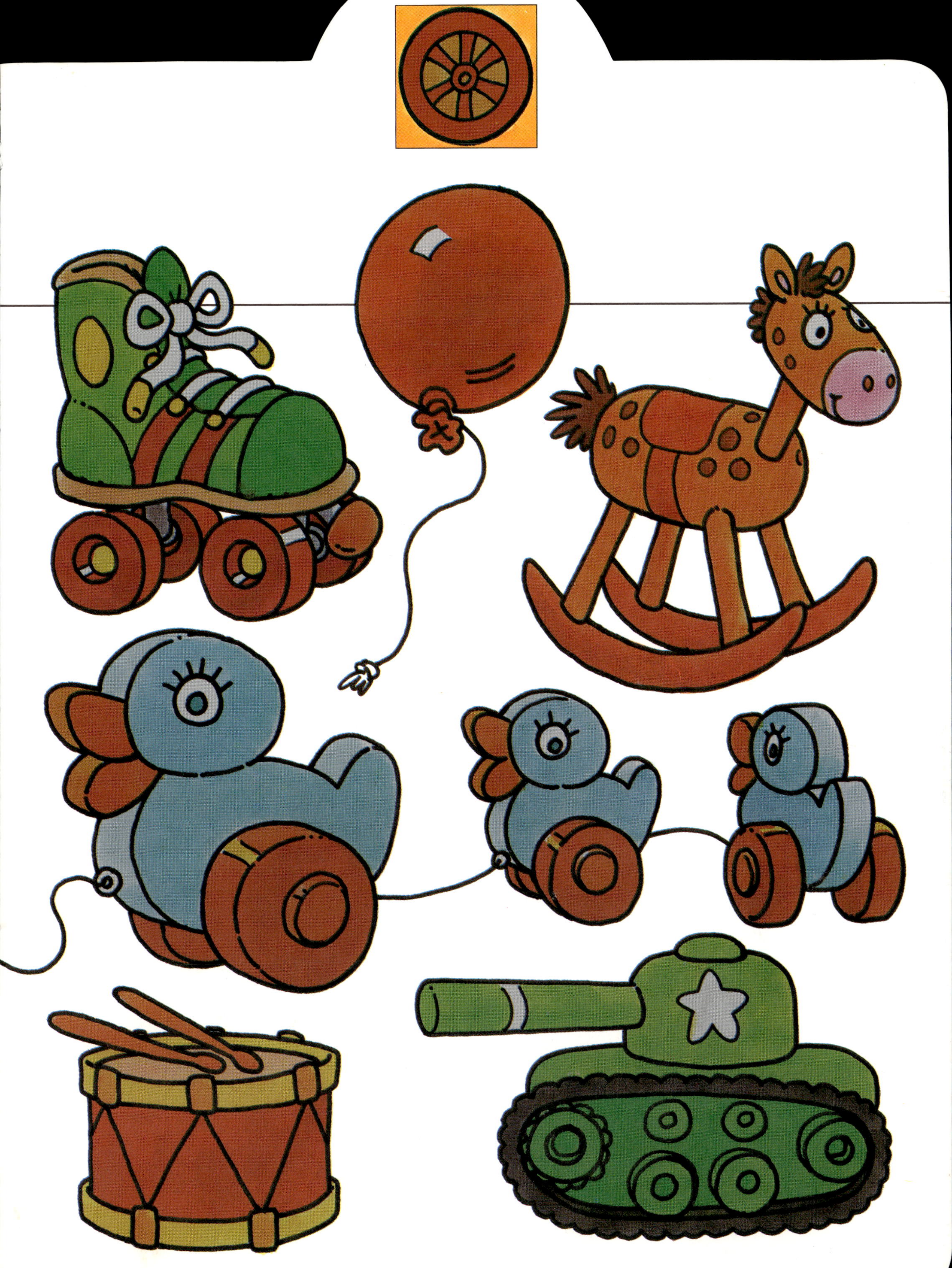

what comes next?

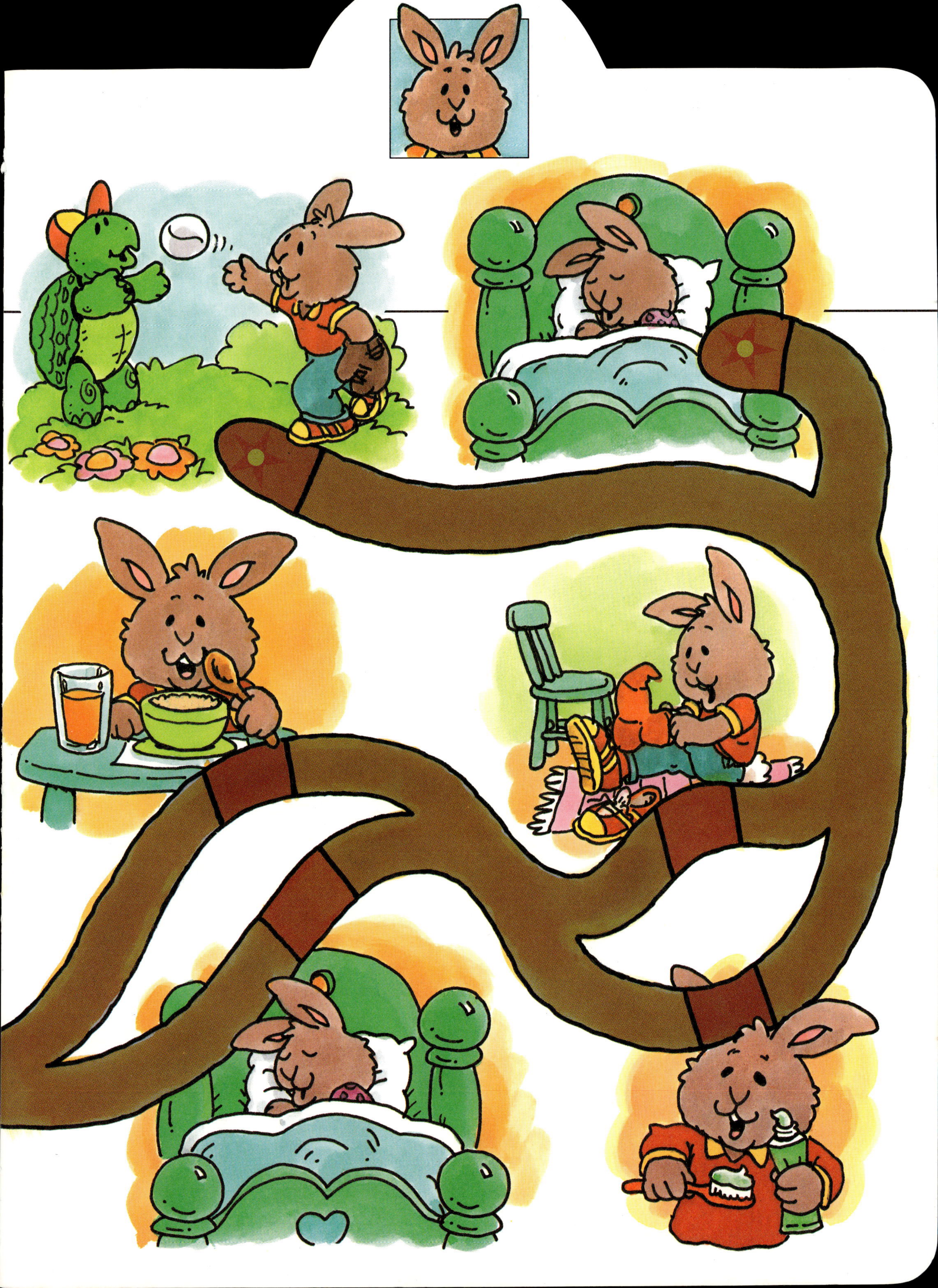

spelling

bat
bot
fat

bag
fall
ball

duke
duck
deer

dog bog fog

bee free tree

hot fat hat

bee bird bat

cot fat cat

which word?

cap
sap
map

bat cat fat

duck
truck
luck

fog dog bog

fall tall ball

tree
dog
bat

bat
cat
rat

hat mat fat

on the table